J. Murray

A sketch of the history of two acts of the Irish Parliament

of the 2d and 8th Queen Anne, to prevent the further growth of popery

J. Murray

A sketch of the history of two acts of the Irish Parliament
of the 2d and 8th Queen Anne, to prevent the further growth of popery

ISBN/EAN: 9783744740630

Printed in Europe, USA, Canada, Australia, Japan

Cover: Foto ©ninafisch / pixelio.de

More available books at **www.hansebooks.com**

A

SKETCH

OF THE

HISTORY

OF

Two Acts of the Irish Parliament, to Prevent the further Growth of Popery.

TO WHICH IS ADDED

THE CIVIL AND MILITARY
ARTICLES OF LIMERICK.

A

SKETCH

OF THE

HISTORY

OF

TWO ACTS OF THE IRISH PARLIAMENT,
THE 2d AND 8th OF QUEEN ANNE,
PREVENT THE FURTHER GROWTH OF POPERY.

IN A

LETTER

TO A

MEMBER

OF THE

HOUSE OF COMMONS IN IRELAND.

TO WHICH ARE ADDED,

THE CIVIL AND MILITARY
ARTICLES OF LIMERICK.

——————— *Hinc illæ Lacrymæ!*

LONDON:

PRINTED, FOR J. MURRAY No. 32. FLEET-STREET.
M DCC LXXVIII.

A

LETTER

TO A

MEMBER of the HOUSE of COMMONS

in IRELAND.

SIR,

IN our late conference on the Popery Laws,
particularly on those of the 2d and
8th of Queen Anne, to prevent the further
growth of Popery in Ireland, you seemed
displeased, that I did not subscribe to your
opinion, " That these laws were not only
" just and equitable in themselves, but also,
" so necessary a barrier to the protestant
" religion, that were they to be relaxed
" or weakened in the smallest degree, Po-

B   pery,

" thoufand pounds fhould be offered for
" apprehendin im, in cafe he landed in
" any part of Ireland."

But there feems to be fomething burlefque,
in bringing the reformation into the above
address

tempt. In their addrefs to the king that year, there are
the following remarkable words: " It is with the utmoft
" concern we find, that this country has been *fo unfortu-*
" *nate as to give birth to James Butler,* late duke of Or-
" mond, a perfon who in defpite of his allegiance, and
" the obligations of *repeated oaths,* has been one of the
" *chief authors* and fomentors of the wicked, and unnatu-
" ral rebellion now begun in Great Britain." Com. Jour.
vol. IV f. 21.

" The Catholics of Ireland," fays a late ingenious writer
on this occafion, " were left to the mercilefs zeal of the
" duke of Ormond, who, *regardlefs of public faith,*
" *and the articles of the capitulation of Limerick,* formed,
" and had enacted a body of penal ftatutes—through which
" there runs fuch a vein of ingenious cruelty, that they feem
" to be dictated by fome prætor of Dioclefian or Spanifh in-
" quifitor, rather than by a Britifh nobleman—The duke
" thought, perhaps, to attone for immoralities, by en-
" tailing mifery on a confiderable part of the Irifh na-
" nation. In his expedition on the coaft of Spain, his fol-
" diers committed many outrages, and profanations of what
" was thought facred by the inhabitants—Yet, after the
" bill of attainder had paffed againft him, he fled for pro-
" tection to *that* country, where he had connived at the
" facrilegious excelfes of his army ; and afterwards retired
" to Aigufin, *a territory belonging to the firft prelate of*
" *that church, which he had treated with fo much cruelty.*"
Confider. on the Penal Laws againft R. Catholics.

addrefs of thanks to his Grace, for having obtained a penal law againft the exercife of the popifh religion. All the world knows that the reformation took its rife from freedom of enquiry, and the right of private judgment: and that the penalties inflicted by the church of Rome, on all who differ from her in doctrine, or difcipline, was one of the principal motives of our quitting her communion; and fhall we pretend to propagate, or fupport the reformed religion, by means that are inconfiftent with thofe, which confeffedly gave birth to the reformation itfelf? Is it right in us to inflict pains and penalties on papifts, for difference of opinion in religious matters, while we upbraid and condemn them, for having formerly inflicted them upon us, on the fame account? muft we give up a fundamental principle of the proteftant religion, and adopt a popifh one, for the defence and propagation of the proteftant religion? and yet, Sir, fuch glaring abfurdity and contradiction will neceffarily follow from our enacting, or executing penal laws, againft the exercife of the popifh religion.

But

But to come to the particular laws in question, so far am I from thinking them just, or equitable in any respect, that I shall endeavour to demonstrate to you, first, that they were consciously framed in violation of the public faith, and against natural right; and secondly, that instead of bringing honour, or support, to our established religion, they have a manifest tendency to weaken, and disgrace it, by dissolving entirely those moral, and religious ties, which christians of all denominations have hitherto believed to be indispensably binding on the consciences of men.*

For this purpose, give me leave, Sir, to remind you, that by the first of the Civil Articles of Limerick (which, upon the surrender of that city, were freely, and solemnly entered into, in the year 1691, with

* That great and eminent lawyer, lord Camden, not long since, took occasion, in the House of Lords, to declare publickly, that these laws " were a heap of monstrous ab- " surdities and vile oppression; subversive of the moral " duties between man and man; and a profanation of " whatever is held most sacred in religion."

with general Ginckle, commander in chief
of their majesties K. William and Q. Mary's
forces in Ireland, in conjunction with the
then lords justices; and afterwards confirmed by the *King and Queen) "It
" was stipulated, and agreed, that *the Ro-*
" *man Catholicks of that kingdom* should enjoy
" such privileges in the exercise of their re-
" ligion, as were confistent with the laws of
" it (then in being) or as they did enjoy in
" the reign of † King Charles II. and that
" their Majesties, as soon as their affairs
" would permit them to summon a parlia-
" ment there, would endeavour to procure
" the said Roman catholicks such *further se-*
" *curity* in that particular, as might preserve
" them

* In their Majesties confirmation of these articles are the
following words: " And as to such parts thereof, for which
" an act of parliament shall be found to be necessary, we
" shall recommend the same to be *made good by parliament,*
" and shall give our royal assent to any bill or bills, that
" shall be passed by our two houses of parliament for that
" purpose."

† In the reign of Charles II. by the laws then in force all
" the papists of Ireland had the same liberty, that any of
" their fellow-subjects had, to purchase any manors, lands,
" tenemets, hereditaments, leases of lives, or for years, or
" any other thing of profit whatsoever."

" them from *any difturbance* on account of
" their religion." And by the eleventh of
the fame articles, " the lords juftices; and
" general Ginckle did undertake to ufe
" their utmoft endeavours, that thefe arti-
" cles fhould be ratified, and confirmed in
" parliament."

This furrender, Sir, of Limerick, and
the other garrifons poffeffed by the Irifh
for King James, happened at a moft favourable conjuncture for King William;
who was then engaged in a war with
France; * a fleet, fent by Lewis XIV.
to the relief of Limerick, having arrived
in Dingle-bay a day or two after the articles were figned; which, had it got fafe up
to the town a day or two before, would have
protracted the Irifh war, to the great difappointment, and obftruction of K. William's foreign defigns. *(f)* " This fleet con-
fifted,

* Harris's life of K. William, f. 353.. " But a few days
" before the furrender of the town, they were encouraged
" by new intelligence of twenty fhips of war fpeedily to arrive
" (from France) under the command of Monfieur Chateau
" Renault." Leland Hift. of Ireld. vol. 3d. p. 610.

(f.) Harris' life of K. William.

" fifted, as appears by the minutes of a letter
" from the lords juftices to the king, of eigh-
" teen fhips of war, fix fire-fhips, and twen-
" ty great veffels of burthen; and brought
" on board between 8 and 10,000 arms, 200
" officers, and 3000 men." I mention thefe
particulars, to fhew you, of how great importance this capitulation was, at that
juncture, to thofe who afterwards thought
it neceffary, for the advancement of the
proteftant religion, to make a public, and
permanent breach, by a law, in the firft
principal article of it.

But the infringement of thefe articles,
on the part of government, commenced
very early after they were figned; and
it was afterwards repeated, from time to
time, in fuch a manner, as prepared the
minds of the people to receive with
lefs furprize, the total violation of them
by the acts to prevent the further growth
of popery, which were even then in con-
templation.

For although by the firft military article, " it was agreed, that all perfons, of
" what quality foever, that were willing

C   " to

" to leave the kingdom, fhould have free
" liberty to go into any country beyond the
" feas (England and Scotland excepted)
" *with their families ;*" yet, it is confefled
that the lords juftices, and general
Ginckle, endeavoured to render this article of as little force as poffible, " for, as
" great numbers of the Irifh officers and
" foldiers had refolved to enter into the.
" fervice of France, and to carry their fa-
" milies with them, Ginckle would not
" fuffer their wives and children to be
" fhipped off with the men ; not doubting
" but that by detaining the former, he
" would have prevented many of the lat-
" ter from going into that fervice." (g) This
I fay, was, confeffedly, an infraction of
that article.

It appears by a letter of the lords juftices
of the 19th of November 1691, not quite
two months after the figning of the articles, " that their lordfhips had received
" complaints from *all parts of Ireland,* of
" the

(g) Harris' life of K. William.

" the * ill treatment of the Irifh who had
" fubmitted, had their majefties protection,
" or were included in articles; and that
" they were fo extremely terrified with ap-
" prehenfions of the *continuance* of that
" ufage, that *fome thoufands* of them, who
" had quitted the Irifh army, and went
" home, with a refolution *not to go* for
" France, were then come back again and
" preft earneftly to go thither, rather than
" ftay in Ireland, where, *contrary to the*
" *publick faith,* (add thefe juftices) *as well*
" *as law, and juftice, they were robbed of*
" *their fubftance, and abufed in their per-*
" *fons."*

The following curious anecdote concerning thefe articles will probably throw fome
light

* About this time, " the juftices of peace, fheriffs, and o-
" ther magiftrates, prefuming on their power in the country,
" had, by colour of their authority, in an illegal and arbi-
" trary manner, difpoffeffed feveral of their majefty's fubjects
" *not only of their goods and chattles,* but of *their lands*
" *and tenements,* to the great difturbance of the peace of
" the kingdom, fubverfion of the law, and reproach of their
" majefty's government. The lords juftices, therefore, com-
" manded fuch practices to be forborn. Harris. Ib. f. 357.

light on the caufe of this early infringement of them. King William, as I have
before obferved, was at this time engaged
in a war with France; but, *(h)* " while his
" troops were divided, by means of the
" Irifh war, he could not proceed, with
" the defired fuccefs, in Flanders; and
" therefore, to put a fpeedy end to that
" war, he fent inftructions to the lords
" juftices to iffue a declaration, affuriug
" the Irifh of *much more favourable conditi-*
" *ons,* than they afterwards obtained by
" the articles of Limerick, the juftices
" formed thefe inftructions into a procla-
" mation, afterwards ftyled the *fecret pro-*
" *clamation,* becaufe though printed, it
" was never publifhed, for their lordfhips
" finding Limerick reduced to the condi-
" tion of capitulating, *fmothered* the pro-
" clamation; and haftened to the camp,
" that they might hold the Irifh to as *hard*
" terms, as the king's affairs would per-
" mit. This they effected, and although
" (adds my *(i)* author) they deferved the
" thankful acknowledgments of every pro-
                                        " teftant

(*h*) Id. ib. f. 372.   (*i*) Ib. ib.

" teftant in the kingdom; yet a party foon
" fprung up that inveighed loudly againft
" the articles. The défigning men of this
" party quarreled with them, only becaufe
" their expectations were difappointed of
" raifing large fortunes out of the forfei-
" tures; but they eafily drew a *majority of*
" *the proteftants* to their fide. They thought
" the Irith entitled to *no articles,* but what
" would expofe them to the fevereft events
" of war. They cenfured the lords juf-
" tices, and the general, as if the king
" and kingdom were betrayed, *infifting that*
" *the articles ought not to be obferved.* This
" party-war was foon declared from the
" pulpit. *(k)* Doctor Dopping, bifhop of
" Meath, preaching before the juftices in
" Chrift-church, the funday after they
" had returned from the camp, argued,
" that the peace ought not to be obferved
" with a people fo * perfidious. To obvi-
ate

(*k*) Id. ib.
* This ill opinion of Irifh papifts was, probably, taken
from thofe fcandalous libels (then induftrioufly publifhed
and propagated) on the principles, and actions of fuch of
thefe people as had been concerned in any of the different
infurrections

" ate this notion, Doctor Moreton, bishop
" of Kildare, the following sunday, shew—
" ed the *obligation* of *keeping the public faith*.
" This matter became so much the subject
" of discourse, that it was necessary to set—
" tle people's opinions on the controverted
                                    " points ;

insurrections anterior to, or coincident with, the late revolution ; and all the penal laws, since enacted against the
exercise of their religion, and the security of their property,
seem to have proceeded from the same cause ; but, besides
that the Irish papists of this day, are not, certainly, accountable for the principles, or actions, of their predecef-
fors ; that the experience of almost a century has proved
them to be good subjects : and that those libels, in which they
are traduced, have been clearly shewn to contain nothing
else, but grofs misreprefentations, or misconstructions, of
facts, the mean but natural, effects of party-zeal and ma-
levolence (see Historic. and Critic. Review of the civil wars
of Ireland) yet some of the most grievous of these penal
laws are still, daily enforced against them. Whereas it is
confefled, that both the principles, and actions of those proteftants, who call themselves anabaptifts, were, originally,
rebellious, sanguinary, and utterly subverfive of all order,
and society (see Dr. Robertfon's life of Charles V. p 348,
&c.) yet, on account of their present peaceable behaviour,
and difpofitions, they are justly indulged in the full protection of the laws of their country, with respect to both their
civil, and religious rights ; and can it be confonant to either
the wifdom, or equity, of government, to treat so very dif-
ferently, two clafles of dutiful subjects, for no other reafon,
but becaufe one of them is called *popifh*, and the other proteftant.

" points; and to that end, Dean Singe,
" preached in the fame church, *keep peace*
" *with all men, if it be poffible*; and mo-
" derated fo *judicioufly, that no more
" was heard of the difpute from the pul-
" pit; but in *parliament and council*, the
" difference fubfifted, until the Englifh
" act of refumption quieted the difputants,
" who then faw they loft nothing by the
" articles."

Thus, Sir, you fee, not only of what importance this furrender of Limerick, and the other garrifons, was to King William, at that period; but alfo, what doctrine was preached from the pulpit, and what opinions were maintained in the council, and parliament, with refpect to the obligation of public faith, when engaged to

Roman

---

* " By afferting" (fays my author) " that *the papifts*
" *were not to be trufted*, but that the articles were to be
performed." Ib. A ftrange way of moderating this! one of
the contracting parties is not to be trufted, and yet the o-
ther is obliged to perform. If prejudice had not blinded the
Preacher, he would have feen that fuch obligations are always mutual, and equally binding on both parties, or not
binding on either.

Roman · Catholics. And that the majority of Proteſtants, in the enſuing Councils, and Parliaments, adhered to Biſhop Dopping's perfidious doctrine, " that the articles of the " Peace ought not to be obſerved with them," will evidently appear · from the conſtant tenour of their ſubſequent proceedings a-gainſt theſe people; a brief ſpecimen of which I am now going to lay before you. ·

It is confeſsed, that ſo early as (l) " the " year 1693, Lord Capel, one of the Lords " Juſtices, proceeded as far as it was in his " power, to *Infringe* the articles of Lime-" rick." In 1695, the ſame Lord Capel, be-ing Deputy, was held the ſecond Seſſion of the firſt Iriſh Parliament, in· this Reign. If the Roman Catholics of Ireland expect-ed, at this Juncture, the performance of the King's ſolemn promiſe, to procure them ſuch further ſecurity from Parliament, as ſhould preſerve them from any future diſ-turbance, on account of their Religion (and ſurely their right to expect it was unqueſ-tionable) they were, indeed miſerably diſ-appointed.

(*l*) Harris Ib. f. 350.

appointed. For, inſtead of performing that promiſe, his Majeſty, on the contrary, ſuffered ſuch acts and * Reſolutions to be paſſed in that Parliament, as gave them infinite Diſturbance, on account of their Religion. But theſe *(m)* " were only preparatory ſteps to the ſeveral acts, *then in agitation, to prevent the further growth of Popery.*" A-
D mong

. (*m*) Id. Ib.

* December 1ſt, 1697. " Reſolved, that part of the Act " 2d Eliz. Chap. 2d. which obliges every perſon, not having " a lawful or reaſonable excuſe to be abſent, to reſort every Sunday to Church, and there abide during the time of common prayer, preaching, and other ſervice of God be there miniſtered, under pain of forfeiting for every neglect, twelve-pence, ought to be put in execution." Comm. Jour. vol. 2d. f. 934. An additional, and much more grevious, penalty, which delinquents incurred by this Act were the cenſures of the Church. " And for the execution thereof (ſays the act itſelf) the Queen's moſt excellent Majeſty, and the Lords Temporal, and the Commons in the preſent Parliament aſſembled, do in God's name, earneſtly, require all Archbiſhops, Biſhops, and other ordinaries, that they ſhall endeavou themſelves to the utmoſt of their knowledge, that the due and true execution thereof may be had throughout their Dioceſes, and charges, as they will anſwer before God for ſuch evils, and plagues, wherewith almighty God may juſtly puniſh his people for neglecting this *good* and *wholeſome* Law. See Com. Jour. vol. 2d. f. 983.

mòng many other severe Laws, then enacted against Catholics, on account of their
Religion, his Majesty gave his Royal assent
to that illiberal act to restrain foreign Edu-
cation, by which it was provided, that, " if
any subjects of Ireland should after that
Session of Parliament, go, or send, any
child, or person, to be educated in any Popish University, College or School; or *in
any private family*, or if such Child should,
by any Popish person, be instructed in the popish Religion ; or, if any subjects of Ireland
should send money, or other things, *towards
the maintenance* of such child, or other person, already sent, or to be sent ; every such
offender, being thereof convicted, should
be *for ever* disabled to sue, or prosecute,
any Action, Bill, Plaint, or Information, in
law, or equity : be incapable of receiving
any legacy, or deed of gift ; or being Guar-
dian, Administrator, or Executor, to any
person.   And besides, that they should *for-
feit all their Estates, both Real and Personal*
during their Lives. " *

Now

* I have not been able, says Mr. Langrishe, in my researches
into Holy writ, to meet with that particular passage of the
scriptures;

Now, Sir, when you confider, not only
the general feverity of this act, but alfo,
that

fcriptures, which gives us an authority to propagate the faith,
by a perverfion of morals, nor fhall I prefume to determine
how far it was *ever* juftifiable, for the fake of ceremo-
nial uniformity, " to build a *Code of Religious laws*, upon
" the ruin of every moral virtue, and obligation ; to fport
" with the moft facred feelings ; to violate the fondeft pre-
" poffeffions of the human mind ; to feduce even filial duty ;
" to tempt the fon to become an Interefted and bafe inform-
" er againft the *piety* of his father ; and to break the bonds
" of all family affection and fidelity." Speech in the Houfe
of Commons 1772, in a debate for enabling Papifts to take
building Leafes.

The chief, if not only objection to the repeal of thefe
Popery Laws, is that it would give the Papifts power and influence. " But fuppofe, fays the fame Mr. Langrifhe, fome
" real and fubftantial influence were to follow from thence ;
" let it be obferved, that the fame caufe which produces this
" influence, does provide againft the ill effects of it, for what
" danger can refult from conferring a degree of power on
" any man, if in the very fame act, and very fame propor-
" tion, you involve his interefts, and affections in the public
" prefervation—Let the Roman Catholics, while they live
" in this country (Ireland) which is the Country of their
" Anceftors, have the ordinary incitements to Induftry, and
" give them a juft and permanent fecurity in their property,
" which will be the fruit of their induftry ; and if after all
" our care. the jealous precautions of the Legiflature fhould
" fo far fail, as that any *Influence* fhould follow in confe-
" quence of fuch fecurity, it is an influence, which, *for their*
" *own fakes*, they will employ in the prefervation of a
                                                    " Country,

that the words " in *any* private family ; or
" by *any* popish perfon," contained in it,
may be conftrued to imply, that even Roman Catholic parents refiding for a time in
a popifh country, and inftructing their children there, in the principles of their religion, are liable, upon their return, to the
penalties of it, you muft certainly confefs,
that, if they fuffered *no difturbance* from
the bare apprehenfion, to fay nothing of
the execution, of this act (which, in that,
and the fucceeding reign, was frequent,
and ftrict) they were, for patience, and
refignation, fome of the beft, and moft
exemplary chriftians, then in the known
world.

It

" Country, which they will then be taught to confider *as
" their own* " — for, " we may reft affured from our know-
" ledge of human nature, from the experience of every na-
" tion in the world, that the *effential Interefts*, not the
" *Speculative opinions*, of men, will be their ultimate con-
" cern ; and that the wifhes, and affections, the hearts
" and the word of every man, will be directed to the de-
" fence of that country, which affords him juftice, tran-
" quility, and protection. "

It is really fhameful to fee, what mean, *
malicious, and frivolous complaints againft
papifts, were received, under the notion of
grievances, by that parliament. (*n*) " A
" petition of one Edward Sprag, and
" others, in behalf of themfelves *and other*
" *proteftant porters*, in and about the city
" of Dublin, complaining that one Dar-
" by Ryan, a *papift*, who dealt in coals,
" employed porters of *his own perfuafion*,
" having been received and read, it was
" ordered to be referred to the *examination*,
" and *confideration* of the *Committee of*
" *Grievances*, and that they fhould report
" their opinion therein to the houfe." It
is obfervable, that the complaint of the
petition was not, that thefe proteftant coal
porters were not employed by Ryan, but
that the popifh coal-porters were.

And yet, Sir, the very fame commons,
that fhewed fuch remarkable deference to
this

---

* November 12th 1696. " Refolved nem. con. that no
" papift be protected by any member of this Houfe, as his
" menial fervant." Com. Jour. vol. 2d. f. 828.

(*n*) Com. Journal vol. 2d. f. 699.

this trifling petition of the proteftant coal-
porters of Dublin, refufed to do common
juftice, in a matter of the laft confequence,
to that of feveral of the moft refpeftable
Roman Catholic gentry of Ireland. For,
upon a bill's being brought into the houfe,
very improperly entitled " an aft for the
" confirmation of the articles of Lime-
" rick," (o) a petition of Robert Cufack,
gentleman, Captain Francis Seagrave, and
Captain Maurice Euftace, in behalf of
themfelves, and others comprized under
the articles of Limerick, fetting forth,
that in the faid bill there were feveral
claufes, that would *fruftrate* feveral parts
of the faid articles, and deprive the petitioners of the benefit of the fame; and, if
paffed, would turn to the *ruin* of fome,
and *prejudice* of all perfons, entitled to the
benefit of faid articles; and praying
to be heard by council to the faid matters,
having been prefented and read, it was *un-
animoufly* refolved, that faid petition fhould
be *rejected.* *

In

(o) Ib. f. 932.
* Although the 6th military article of Limerick exprefsly
provides,

In the fame feffion, (p) " it was refolved, *nemine contradicente,* that the ex-
cluding of papifts from having votes for
the electing of members to ferve in parliament was neceffary to be made into a *
Law," nothing, certainly, but fuch a
law was wanting, to complete the flavery
of thefe people, beyond all poffibility of
redemption. And yet thefe, and feveral
other proceedings of the like enflaving
tendency, were permitted and countenanced by a prince, the boafted reftorer of
liberty to thefe kingdoms, whofe public
faith, and honour, were folemnly engaged,
to preferve their former priviledges entire,
and to endeavour to obtain, from Parliament,

(p) Ib. f. 978.

provides, " that no perfon whatfoever fhall be molefted for
" any wafte, or trefpafs, by him committed *during the late*
" *war* ;" yet on pretence that the bridge of Lanefborough
was broken down by the papifts under K. James, in that
war, a " Bill was ordered into the Houfe of Commons,
" October 1703, for charging the eftates of papifts, *reftor-*
" *ed by the articles of Limerick,* with the expence of re-
" building it." Com. Jour. vol. 3d. f. 87.

* Yet afterwards in the feffion of 1709, in a debate on a
difputed election, fome members infifted, that papifts had a
right to vote in fuch cafes. See Com. Jour. vol. 3d. f. 659.

ment, further Security for them, in the article of religion, which was what alone rendered them obnoxious to government:

I know you will tell me, in vindication of your admired hero King William, that no general good has been ever wrought, without the con-comitance of some evil, done to particulars; that in politics, as in war, deceit may be fometims lawful : that äs K. William's fole defign in coming into thefe kingdoms was to refcue us out of the jaws of thofe two formidable monfters, popery and flavery, then ready to devour us (which he has effectually done) gratitude for our deliverance ought to make us overlook, and forget, whatever might appear to the eye of bigotry, not ftrictly juftifiable, in the execution of it. To which I anfwer, not only that it is not clear, that that Prince's *fole* defign in coming into thefe kingdoms, was to refcue us from the two formidable monfters you mention; but alfo that it is highly probable, after he had fully attained his principal end in coming, that he privately engaged to expofe

pofe us to that fuppofed danger, by pro-
mifing to re-eftablifh the abdicated family
on the throne of Great Britain, after his
own deceafe. Of the grounds of this probability you will be able to judge, by the
following fecret tranfaction, which has
been but lately brought to light.

(*a*) " In the treaty of peace at *Ryfwick,*
" as King William trufted not his three
" plenipotentiaries with his agreement with
" France, mankind juftly concluded, that
" a fecret of the laft importance had been
" for fome time depending between the
" two kings; time has at length unravel-
" led *the myftery*. Lewis, unwilling to de-
" fert James, propofed, that the Prince of
" Wales, the Pretender, fhould fucceed to
" the crown of England, *after the death of*
" *William*. The King, *with little hefitation,*
" agreed to the requeft: he *even folemnly en-*
" *gaged* to procure *the repeal of the Act of*
" *fettlement* : and to declare by another act,
" *the Prince of Wales his fucceffor to the*
" *throne :* thofe (adds my author) who
E " afcribe

(*a*) Macpherfon's Hiftory of England.

" afcribe all the actions of William to pu-
" blic fpirit, will find fome difficulty in
" reconciling this tranfaction to their ele-
" vated opinion of his character. In this
" one conceffion to France, he yielded up
" all his profeffions to England; and by an
" act of indifcretion, or through indiffe-
" rence, deferted the principles to which
" he owed the throne."

It would be irkfome to recite the many*
other inftances of the breach of thefe articles, which we find recorded in the Jour-
nals of that parliament. I fhall therefore,
only mention one remarkable paffage, which
immediately preceded the paffing of this
" juft,

* Though by the 9th civil article of Limerick, the oath
to be tendered to Roman Catholics, to entitle them to all
the privileges, and benefits of thefe articles, was the oath
of fidelity or allegiance to their Majefties, and *no other;*
yet it was " refolved, nem. con. in November 1697, that
" fome *further* oath, than what was required *by law*, re-
" nouncing the *Papal* authority in this kingdom, is necef-
" fary for the peace, and quiet thereof." Com. Jour. vol.
III. f. 979, and indeed, what a variety of other captious
oaths has been fince devifed, to enfnare and corrupt the confciences of Papifts, for the only purpofe of propagating and
maintaining a religion, which is faid to owe its very being
to the freedom, and integrity of confcience!

" juſt, and equitable" law, (as you are pleaſed to call it) to prevent the further growth of Popery.

The Roman Catholic citizens of Limerick thought themſelves particularly * ſecured by their articles from any future moleſtation, on account of their religion, but, beſides what they had already ſuffered, in common with the reſt of their countrymen of the ſame perſuaſion, they are now compelled to abandon their dwellings and ſettlements there, *on that ſingle account*, for, (*b*) " upon a petition of the mayor, ſheriffs, " and *Proteſtant* aldermen of that city com- " plaining" (like the proteſtant coal-porters of Dublin before-mentioned) " that " they were greatly *damaged in their trade*, " and calling, by *the great numbers* of pa- " piſts reſiding there, and praying to be " re-

---

* By the 2d civil article, " the inhabitants, or reſidents " of Limerick, — of what profeſſion, *trade*, or *calling ſoever they be*, ſhall, and may uſe, exerciſe, and practiſe their ſeveral and reſpective trades and callings, as freely as they did uſe, exerciſe, and enjoy the ſame in the reign of King Charles the II.

(*b*) Com. Jour. vol. III. f. 84.

" relieved therein ; a claufe was ordered to
" be inferted in the act to prevent the fur-
" ther Growth of Popery, that every perfon
" of the Popifh Religion, then inhabiting
" within the faid city, or its fuburbs, fhould
" give in *fufficient bail, or fecurity*, before
" the chief magiftrate of the faid city, that
" they would bear themfelves faithfully
" towards her Majefty; or, in default of
" giving *fuch fecurity*, fhould depart out of
" the faid city, and fuburbs." *

Now,

* The act itfelf fets forth, " that if any perfon or perfons
" of the Popifh Religion, other than fuch trading mer-
" chants, *not exceeding twenty in each of the faid towns*
" (Limerick and Galway) as fhall be licenfed by the chief
" governor or governors of this kingdom for the time being,
" fhall prefume to live, dwell, or inhabit, or take any
" houfe or tenement in, the city of Limerick or town of
" Galway, or the fuburbs of either—he, or they, fhall for-
" feit all his or their go 's and chattles, and fuffer impri-
" fonment for the fpace of one whole year." Com. Jour.
vol. iii. f. 132. Sir Theobald Buttler, in his pleading a-
gainft this bill before the Houfe of Commons, in 1703, ob-
ferves, " that the Roman Catholic citizens of Limerick were
" prohibited by it from living or ftaying there, *even fuch*
" *as were under the articles*, and by virtue thereof, had
" ever fince lived there, without giving fuch fecurity, as
" neither thefe articles, nor any law heretofore in force, do
" require,

Now, Sir, befides the difficulty of their getting fuch fecurity, as, at that period of jealoufy and diftruft, would be allowed *fufficient* by the chief magiftrate, who was himfelf the *principal petitioner* againft them: even thofe few Popifh inhabitants, whofe fecurity was unexceptionable, and who, confequently, could not be hindred to continue in their habitations, were yet, foon after, put under a neceffity of abandoning them, of their own accord: unlefs it can be fuppofed, that trading people can live contentedly, or with any fort of convenience, in a place, where they are forced to remain feparate from their wives, children, and fervants; for that fuch was to be the fituation of thofe *few* licenfed papifts (not more than twenty were fuffered to be licenfed) is manifeft from hence, that, "in (*a*) March 1704, a petition from the "Roman Catholic inhabitants of Lime-"rick, praying that *bail* might be taken "for their wives, children, and fervants, "*as inhabitants thereof,* having been pre-
"fented

"require, except feamen, fifher-men, and day labourers, "who did not pay above forty fhillings a year, rent."
(*a*) Ib. f. 281.

" fented to the houfe, and read, it was
" ordered to be *rejected*."

It is worthy of particular notice, that
about the time of paſſing this act to prevent
the further growth of popery, feveral members of the Houfe of Commons, as if a-
fhamed of having been any way concerned
in that tranfaction, refigned their feats;
defiring that writs might be iſſued to
chufe other members in their room. And
this humour of refigning became fo general among them, that it was (*b*) (at laft)
" unanimouſly refolved, that it might be
" made the *ſtanding order of the houfe,* that
" no new writs for electing members of
" parliament, in the place of members *ex-*
" *cuſing themſelves* from the fervice of the
" houfe, do iſſue *at the defire* of fuch mem-
" bers, notwithſtanding any former prece-
" dent to the contrary." *

Upon

(*h*) Com. Jour. vol. III. f. 296. It had been before refolv-
" ed, that the excuſing of members *at their own requeſt*, from
" the fervice of the Houfe, and thereupon iſſuing out new
" writs to elect other members, to ferve in their places, was
" of dangerous confequence, and tended to the *ſubverſion*
" of the conſtitution of parliament."

* The fecond Act to prevent the further **Growth** of Popery,

Upon the return of this bill to prevent the further Growth of Popery, from England, (*a*) " Nicholas Lord Kingsland, Col. " John Brown, Col. Burke, Col. Robert " Nugent, Major Allen, Capt. Arthur " French, with other Roman Catholics of " Ireland, and persons comprised in the " articles of Limerick and Galway, peti- " tioned to be heard by council against " it : which was granted."

This returned bill had a clause inserted in England, which gave great offence to the whole body of dissenters in Ireland : many of whom, then in the House of Commons, were persons of considerable power and influence; for this reason, it was expected, that it would have been totally laid aside; and the rather, because the dissenters had before received some disgust, by a resolution of a committee in October 29th, 1703, (*b*) " that the pen- " sion of 1200 l. per ann. granted to the presbyterian

---

pery, was under debate in the House of Commons, from the 10th of May 1709, to the 18th of June following. See Com. Jour. from f. 575, to f. 641.

(*a*) Ib. f. 173.　　　(*b*) Com Jour. vol. I.I. f. 76.

" prefbyterian minifters in Ulfter, was an
" *unneceffary* branch of the eftablifhment."

The diffenters, in their petition to the
Commons, on occafion of the above-
mentioned claufe, complained, " that, to
" their *great furprife aud difappointment,*
" they found a claufe inferted in the Act
" to prevent the further growth of Popery,
" which had not its rife in that honoura-
" ble houfe, whereby they were difabled
" from executing any public truft, for the
" fervice of her majefty, the proteftant
" religion, or their country, unlefs *contra-*
" *ry to their confciences,* they fhould receive
" the Lord's Supper, according to the
" rites and ufages of the eftablifhed
" church."*

This claufe has fince been called the fa-
cramental teft, then firft impofed on the
diffenters of Ireland, whofe zeal againft Popery was fo creduloufly blind, that upon a
promife of having it repealed on the firft
opportunity,

---

* Prefbyterian loyalty *fub finem*, notwithftanding their
having fince made many ftrenuous efforts for its repeal.——
Nec lex eft juftior ulla, quam necis artifices arte perire fua.

opportunity, they readily concurred with the reſt in paſſing (together with the clauſes again Popery) that mortifying one againſt themſelves; which as a juſt judgment for ſuch concurrence, has remained in full force againſt them ever ſince. *

On the 23d of February 1703, purſuant to leave given by the Commons, Sir Theobald Buttler, Councellor Malone, and Sir Stephen Rice (the two former in their gowns, as council fur the petitioners in general, and the laſt without a gown, as only petitioner in his private capacity) appeared at the bar of the Houſe of Commons. Sir Theobald Butler, the firſt, and principal ſpeaker on this occaſion, demon-

F   ſtrated,

---

* This clauſe, inſtead of being repealed, was afterwards frequently put in ſtrict execution during Queen Anne's reign. "October 29th 1707, reſolved, that by an act to prevent "the farther Growth of Popery, the burgeſſes of *Belfaſt* are "obliged to ſubſcribe the declaration, and receive the ſa- "crament, according to the uſage of the church of Ireland." Reſolved, "that the burgeſhip of the ſaid burgeſſes of "Belfaſt, who had not ſubſcribed the declaration, and re- "ceived the ſacrament *purſuant to the ſaid act*, were by "ſuch neglect, become *vacant*." - Com. Jour. vol. III. f. 546.

ftrated, in a long and pathetic fpeech, that almoft every claufe in the Act then before them, relating to the Roman Catholics of Ireland, was a direct infringement of one or other of the articles of Limerick, which he at the fame time held in his hand, " ar-" ticles," added he, " folemnly engaged " to them, as the public faith of the na-" tion—that all the Irifh then in arms " againft the government, had fubmitted " thereunto, and furrendered the city of " Limerick, and all other garrifons in their " poffeffion ; when they were *in a condition* " *to have held out*, till they might have " been relieved, *by the fuccours then coming* " out of France: that they had taken fuch " oaths to the King and Queen, as by the " fame articles, they were obliged to take : " that their fubmiffion was upon fuch " terms, as ought to be then, and at all " times, made good to them; and that " therefore, to break thofe articles, would " be the greateft injuftice for any one peo-" ple in the whole world to inflict upon " ano-

(*a*) Ib. f. 279. (*b*) Account of the debates on the Popery Laws.

" another, being contrary to laws both of
" God and * man: that the cafe of the
" Gibeonites, 2 Sam. xxi. 1. was a fear-
" ful example of the breach of public
" faith; which, above a hundred years
" after, brought nothing lefs than a three
" years famine on the land, and ftayed not
" untill the lives of all Saul's family attoned
" for it. That even among the heathens,
" and moft barbarous nations all the world
" over, the public faith was always held
" facred and binding; and that, furely,
" it would find no lefs regard, in that af-
" fembly."

" The

---

* Of the law of gavel kind, (enacted by the 18th claufe
of this bill) Sir Theobald Butler in his pleadings fays, it is
" a law in itfelf, *fo monftrous*, that I dare fay this is the
" *firft time* it was ever heard of in the world"——" for
" furely, adds he, it is a ftrange law, which contrary to
" the laws of all nations, thus confounds all fettlements,
" how ancient foever, or otherwife warrantable by all the
" laws hitherto in force, in this, or any other kingdom."
" Informers are an infamous and odious fet of people, and
" in fact, the Irifh Popery laws, and the conftruction put
" upon them by the Irifh lawyers and courts of juftice, are a
" confufed heap of oppreffion and nonfenfe, and have very
" much contributed to corrupt the morals of the people of
" that country." Lord Chancellor Camden, in the Houfe
of Lords, February 9th 1775.

The fame, and other arguments, againſt the paſſing of this bill, were ſuffered to be pleaded at the bar of the Houſe of Lords; but were equally diſregarded by both Houſes: the petitioners were told, (*a*) " that, if they were to be deprived of the " benefits of the articles of Limerick, it " would be their own faults, ſince *by com-* " *forming to the eſtabliſhed religion*, they " would be entitled to theſe, and many " other benefits: and that, therefore, they " ought not to blame any but themſelves, " that the paſſing of that bill *was needful* " *for the ſecurity of the kingdom*; and that " there was *nothing in the articles of Lime-* " *rick, that ſhould hinder them to paſs it.*"

The former part of this anſwer, Sir, was, you ſee, downright mockery, and a public inſult on national faith; and, by the latter, a maxim ſeems to have been adopted, which tends to deſtroy all truſt and confidence among men, viz. that the moſt ſolemn engagement between parties may be violated or ſet aſide, by either of

them,

(*a*) Ib.

them, upon a feigned or groundlefs apprehenfion of danger from the other, by
keeping it. I call the apprehenfion of
danger, in this cafe, feigned or groundlefs,
becaufe I think, I may challenge the ableft,
and moft zealous fticklers for thefe laws, to
produce even one inftance of fuch mifcon-
duct of the Roman Catholics of Ireland,
from the year 1691, when the articles of
Limerick were concluded, to the year
1704, when the firft of thefe laws was
paffed, as could occafion in the government
any real or grounded apprehenfion of danger
or difturbance from them. That no fuch inftance could be then produced, appears from
hence, that one of the principal objections
to their conduct was, * " their not having
" congratulated

---

* Ib. Through this whole reign great numbers of Roman
Catholics quitted the kingdom, on account of the fevere
execution of the Popery Laws ; and fuch as were willing to
return were not permitted, without licenfe obtained on the
hardeft terms. In 1713, " ordered to prepare an addrefs
" to her majefty, to defire her, that fhe will be pleafed not
" to grant licenfes to Papifts to return into this kingdom."
Com. Jour. vol. III. It was even dangerous for them to
attempt, or endeavour to hear what paffed in the Houfe of
Commons concerning themfelves; for in the fame year, an
order was paffed, " that the ferjeant at arms fhould take
" into cuftody all Papifts that were or fhould prefume to
" come into the galleries." Ib. f. 976.

" congratulated her Majesty Queen Anne,
" by a dutiful addrefs, on her acceffion to
" the throne, as her Proteftant fubjects had
" done;" which as it may be reafonably
accounted for, from their depreffed, per-
fecuted, and defponding condition at that
juncture ; fo, had they actually addreffed
her Majefty on that occafion, in the moft
loyal and affectionate manner, moft probable it is, that their very accufers would
have confidered and reprefented it, as the
mere effect of adulation and hypocrify, if
not of infolence and prefumption in them.

Perfons, who are confcious of having often, and openly, broken faith with others,
have reafon to dread, that others will not be
fcrupuloufly exact in keeping faith with them.
It was, perhaps, from fuch confcioufnefs,
that the government of Ireland, during all
Queen Anne's reign, were inceffantly ham-
pering the Roman Catholics with oaths,
imprifonments, and forfeitures, without
any other vifible caufe, but that of their
* Religion. But ·the behaviour of thefe
people

* What pitiful occafions were then taken, to perfecute
the perfons of Roman Catholics from every trifling act, or
circumftance

people was always found fo blamelefs, that
it fometimes made their very perfecutors
afhamed of their feverity. In the year
1708, on the bare rumor of an intended In-
vafion *of Scotland* by the pretender, no few-
er than (*b*) "*forty one Roman Catholic Noble-*
"*men and Gentlemen* were imprifoned in
"the Caftle of Dublin." (*c*) And when
they

circumftance, of their Religion. appears from the following
paffage among many others. There is, it feems, a place of
Pilgrimage with them, in the county of Meath, called St.
John's well, which is frequented every fummer, moftly by
infirm men, women, and children, in hopes of being cured
of their feveral diforders, by performing certains acts of
devotion, and penance there. This the Irifh Commons
thought an important object of confideration, and of national concern ; and accordingly paffed a vote, that thefe
fickly devotees "were affembled there, to the great hazard,
" and *danger* of the public peace, and *fafety of the king-*
" *dom.*" In confequence of which, fines, imprifonment,
and whipping, were made the penalties of " fuch dange-
" rous, and tumultuous, affemblies." A penance, much
more fevere, than thofe poor people probably intended to inflict on themfelves ; and from which, they could hardly obtain any other cure of their diforders but that univerfal one
death ; which in thofe times of religious rancour, frequently
happened, by the extreme rigor of their punifhment. Com.
Jour. vol. IV.

(*b*) Com. Jour. vol. IV. f. 371. (*c*) Ib.

they were afterwards fet at Liberty, † ("be-
" caufe they had acted nothing againſt the
" Government,") the ſtate was ſo ſenſible
of the wrong done them, by their long,
and irkſome confinement, ‡" that it re-
" mitted their fees, though they amounted
" *to eight hundred and odd pounds.*"

Soon after the firſt act to prevent the further growth of popery was paſſed, the commons entered into ſuch wild, and intem-
perate reſolutions concerning the execution
of it, and of other penal ſtatutes, which it
revives, and confirms, as ſhew them to have
been as little directed by common ſenſe, as
they were by common humanity. In
March 1704 (d) " they reſolved, unani-
" mouſly, that all Magiſtrates, *and other*
" *perſons whatſoever,* who neglected, or o-
" mitted, to put them in due execution,
" *were betrayers of the Liberties of the King-*
" *dom.*" In June 1705, (e) " that the ſay-
" ing, or *hearing*, of Maſs, by perſons who
had

† Ib. ‡ Ib. (*d*) Com. Jour. vol. III. f. 289. (*e*) Ib. 319.

" had not taken the oath of abjuration,
" *tended to advance the interest of the pre-*
" *tender ;* " And, *(f)* " that such *judges,* and
" Magiſtrates, as willfully neglected to
" make diligent *enquiry into* and *diſcover,*
" *ſuch wicked practices,* ought to be looked
" upon as enemies to her Majeſty's Govern-
" ment." And left the Judges at leaſt, if
not the other Magiſtrates, ſhould be ſome-
what aſhamed of executing this new office
of *enquiring into,* and *diſcovering,* theſe wick--
ed practices of ſaying and hearing maſs, on
account of that infamy, which is commonly annexed to the trade of Prieſt-Catchers,
diſcoverers, and informers, theſe commons
had before taken care, " to reſolve *unani-*
" *mouſly,* that the proſecuting, and *informing*
" *againſt Papiſts,* was an * HONOURABLE
G   " ſervice

(ƒ) Ib. 289.

* The ſcheme of the original framers of theſe popiſh
Laws, (and of the preſent advocates for their continuance)
was, and is, by their ſeverity, to baniſh the popiſh natives
out of the Kingdom, and introduce foreign proteſtants, in
their room. This experiment was tried in the year 1709,
" for, at the requeſt of the Lords and others of the council,
" *eight*

"fervice to the Government." Such was
the good faith, good fenfe, and avowed
honour, of thefe bigotted times.

How very different from this, Sir, has
been the ftate and condition of the proteftants in Germany, ever fince the famous
Treaty of Munfter in 1648; which was
concluded with them by the Emperor Fer-
dinand, on a like ftipulation for Liberty of
religious worfhip; and guarantied by *their
moft Chriftian, and Catholic Majefties, and o-
ther*

"eight hundred and twenty one proteftant palatine families
"were then brought over to Ireland; and the fum of twenty
"four thoufand, eight hundred, and fifty pounds, five fhil-
"lings and fixpence, appointed for their maintenance, out
"of the revenue; on a refolution of the Commons," *that
"it would much contribute to the fecurity of the Kingdom,*
"if the faid proteftant palatines were encouraged, and fettled
"therein." But the error of that policy was foon after
"difcovered; for the Lords, in their addrefs to the Queen,
"in 1711, thankfully obferve, "that her Majefty's *early*
"care had even *prevented their own endeavours,* to free the
"nation from that *load of debt,* which the bringing over
"numbers of *ufelefs, and indigent, Palatines* had brought
"upon them." It is remarkable, that only four out of this
great number of proteftant palatines enlifted in her Majefty's army; fuch was the fecurity, which the Kingdom
received from them! fee Com. Jour. vol. III. f. 879. at
this time great numbers of Roman Catholics had been dri-
ven out of Ireland by the feverity of thefe Laws.

ther *Roman Catholic Princes, and states in
Italy, and Germany.* (g) " By this treaty,
"all their immunities, lands, territories, and
" dignities, together with the abfolutely
" free, and uncontrouled exercife of their
" Religion : as alfo powers to bear Offices,
" and enjoy not only Church-Livings, but
" Bifhopricks. and Archbifhopricks, were
" granted, and for ever fecured to thefe
" proteftants : notwithftanding the Pope's
" Nuncio, then prefent at Munfter, openly
" protefted againft it ; and the Pope him-
" felf, Innocent X. foon after iffued a Bull
" declaring its *Nullity,* but this declarati-
" on from the Pope (adds my Author) fig-
" nified no more than one from *Prefter John*
" would have done. The Emperor, and
" Princes of Germany glorioufly ftood to
" their Treaty ; and took care to fee the
" fame folemnly † ratified, and executed,
                    " notwithftanding

(*g*) See Sir Peter Pet. Happy ftate of England. pref.

† " From hence " (adds Sir Peter Pet) " It appears, *how
" unftudied thofe men are in the great Book of the world,*
" who think that popifh Princes will not go on in the courfe
                                                    " of

" notwithſtanding this declaration of its
" nullity. They knew the Pope's nuncio
" would ſoon proteſt, and the Pope him-
" ſelf declare, againſt the Peace ; and there-
" fore, had *in terms agreed* therein, " that
" no *canons*, or *decrees of Councils*, or con-
" cordates

" of their Politics, *though the Pope ſhould ſeem in earneſt,*
" *or in jeſt to ſtop them.*" Ib. Let me add, that although
it be notorious that papal decrees and bulls, touching temporal matters, have been often overlooked, or rejected, by
Roman Catholic Princes, and States, as in the preſent in-
ſtance ; yet there are ſome proteſtants, who merely through
hatred of the religion and perſons of Roman Catholics, not
content with theſe People's abjuring all civil power, and ju-
riſdiction of Popes, in theſe Kingdoms ; inſiſt alſo upon their
abjuring the Pope's ſpiritual power ; which is in no reſpect
whatever concerned in temporal, or political affairs : at the
ſame time that they aſſume a ſuperior ſpiritual power to themſelves, in what they call their chriſtian Liberty of interpret-
ing the word of God (which is not controulable by any
earthly authority) in their own ſenſe, in *matters relative to*
civil as well as religious government, which is likely to
prove much more dangerous, than any ſpiritual authority of
the Pope, to proteſtant Kingdoms and States ; it being evi-
dent from Hiſtory, that the prepoſterous exerciſe of that
power, has principally occaſioned all the rebellions, that have
ariſen in Europe ever ſince the Reformation. For factions,
confuſions, and rebellion, are the natural conſequences of
ſuch falſe notions of chriſtian Liberty : which Mr. Adams, in
his celebrated oration at Philadelphia, in Auguſt 1776, thus
artfully

" *cordates with Popes, or absolutions,* should,
" in any future time, be allowed against
" any article of it." And accordingly, Sir,
" it has been, ever since, religiously ob-
" served, in every particular: and, in all
" probability, will continue to be so.

Thus, instead of the Pope's annulling,
by his bull, the Munster peace *with effect,*
and

artfully enforces, to his American fellow Rebels, as an ar-
gument on which the lawfulness of their insurrection is principally founded. " Our forefathers, says he, threw off the yoke
" of *Popery in Religion* ; for you is reserved the honour of
" *levelling the popery of Politics.* They opened the Bible
" to all, and maintained the *capacity of every man to judge*
" *for himself in Religion.* Are we sufficient for *the com-*
" *prehension of the sublimest spiritual truths,* and *unequal*
" *to material and temporal ones ? Heaven hath trusted us*
" with the management of *things for eternity,* and man de-
" nies us ability to judge of the present, or to know from our
" feelings and experience what will make us happy"—"you
" can discern, say they, objects distant and remote, but can-
" not perceive those within your grasp " — " let us have
" the destribution of present goods, and cut out, and ma-
" nage as you please the interest of futurity" — " This
" day, I trust, *the reign of Political Protestantism* will com-
" mence. We have explored the Temple of Royalty, and
" found that *the Tool we have bowed down to* has eyes
" which see not, ears that hear not our prayers, and a
" heart like the neither mill-stone."

and thereby fixing on the papifts the odious, imputed doctrine " of not keeping " faith with proteftants," you fee that doctrine itfelf was *annulled* in this inftance, by the popifh princes of France, Spain, and Germany, and I will venture to add, that it is now actually reverfed, and may be fairly retorted on their accufers, for the violation of the articles of Limerick.

Need I inform you, Sir, that thefe laws, under the fpecious pretence of preventing the growth of Popery, have, in reality, more effectually, prevented the growth of every thing, that is either ufeful or ornamental, to Ireland; that, inftead of promoting true religion, and its genuine effects, private and public virtue, they have given birth to *more hypocrify*; and under that dangerous difguife, to more of every other fpecies of moral evil, and turpitude, than was before known in this, or any other part of the Chriftian world—that, by thefe laws, great rewards are, occafionally, held forth to that vile and detefted race of men, *difcoverers* and *informers*; who being

thus

thus *legally* countenanced, and encouraged, plunder, indiscriminately, parents, brethren, kinsmen, and friends; in despight of all the ties of blood, of affection, and confidence; in breach of the divine laws, and of all former human laws, enacted in that, or any other kingdom, for the security of property, since the creation of the world.*

You

* The only plausible reason I ever heard for making and continuing these laws, is their tendency to bring the Papists of Ireland to a conformity in religion and loyalty with Protestants; and to weaken and impoverish such of them as had forfeited at the revolution, to so great a degree, that neither they nor their posterity should be ever after capable of giving us any disturbance, in either our civil or religious concerns. As for the first part of this reason, it is notorious, that hypocrisy and disaffection to both our religion and government are the first, and natural effects of such forced conversions; and should even converts, thus made, become at length real Protestants, and good subjects. " Is " evil to be done, that good may arise therefrom," in this one instance, when both reason and religion forbid it in every other ?—As for the second part, the enacting such predatory laws against Papists, without some overt-act, or proof of their intention at least, even at that juncture, to disturb the government, (which is not even pretended) was by no means justifiable. An enemy might compare such
proceeding

You have feen, Sir, that one of the principal caufes affigned for enacting thefe laws againft Roman Catholics, was their not having addreffed Queen Anne, on her acceffion to the throne: that caufe, frivolous as it then was, cannot, now, be affigned for their continuance. Thefe people, Sir, have often fince, and with much better reafon, expreffed their heart-felt gratitude for the lenity fhewn them by that Queen's illuftrious fucceffors, the prefent Royal Family, in humble and dutiful addreffes, which have been gracioufly received. But even thefe addreffes have been malicioufly, becaufe confcioufly, mifreprefented. "The profeffions of loyalty, "and even folemn oaths of Papifts (fay "their enemies) to Proteftant governors, "are infincere and infidious. They are "licenced to make them, but with no "other view, than to propagate their fu- "perftition, and fupplant the true reli- "gion; and when thefe purpofes can be "ferved

proceeding to the policy of an highway-man, in putting thofe he had robbed to death, leaft, if fuffered to live, they might afterwards difcover, and profecute him for the robbery.

" ved by acting counter to them, they
" have difpenfations and abfolutions at a
" call."*

Thus do thefe doughty advocates for
perfecution pretend to more wifdom and
folicitude for the public fafety, than the
Legiflature itfelf: which, in propofing the
ufual oaths to thefe people, have hitherto
imagined, that they were providing for
the fecurity of government, and attaching
them to it, by the ftrongeft ties that can
poffibly bind the confciences of men.
Whereas, it feems, that by receiving them
on fuch terms, into any degree of truft and
confidence, they were giving government's
greateft enemies the beft opportunity they

H   could

* So ridiculoufly jealous and fearful were the framers of
the Acts to prevent the further growth of Popery, of thefe
papal difpenfations and abfolutions, that they obliged the
very *Quakers* to declare againft them, " and folemnly to
" profefs and teftify they made that declaration with any
" difpenfation *already granted by the Pope*, or hope of its
" *being hereafter granted,* and without believing that the
" Pope could *abfolve* them from that declaration." Com·
Jour.

could have defired, for undermining and betraying it.

But can you, Sir, really believe, that men born with the fame feelings, appetites, and paffions, as ourfelves; and confcious too, that they could have obtained difpenfations and abfolutions, at a call, for conforming to the eftablifhed worfhip, would have voluntarily fuffered, during thefe feventy years paft, what all the world knows the Roman Catholics of Ireland have fuffered, on account of their non-conformity, in that fpace of time ? I will not believe you capable of thinking fuch nonfenfe.

The ftraining of confcience for worldly advantages, to make it conform outwardly to modes of religious worfhip, which it inwardly condemns, is a practice unheard of among Roman Catholics ; *occafional conformity*, Sir, a principle avowed by fome of their moft violent accufers, is utterly renounced by them; and they have ever declared themfelves ready to abjure, in the moft folemn manner, all power on earth,
                                           fpiritual

'fpiritual and temporal, fuppofed to be capable of difpenfing with them, in that refpect.*

Thefe

* But of all the evil tenets imputed to Roman Catholics,
as peculiar and effential to their religion, the *fpirit of perfecution* feems moft to be dreaded, and is moft confidently infifted
upon ; but how can fuch a fpirit be deemed peculiar to
Roman Catholics, when it is notorious, that their very accufers perfecute both them, and one another, whenever
they have the power and opportunity of doing it ? that it
is far from being effential to their religion, appears from
hence, that their ableft and moft orthodox divines, and in
particular, their laft Pope, Clement XIV. (who furely muft
be fuppofed to have known the *effentials* of his religion)
condemns it as unchriftian, and inhuman. " The great
" misfortune in this cafe is," fays that eminently good and
learned Prelate, " that fome people *confound religion with*
" *her minifters*, and make *her refponfible for their faults* ;
" it never was religion, but falfe zeal pretending to imitate
" her, that feized fire and fword, to compel heretics to ab-
" jure their errors, and Jews to become Chriftians. There
" were formerly (he confeffes) in the bofom of the church
" falfe zealots, who contended for things not interefting to
" the faith ; of whom (adds he) Ecclefiaftical Hiftory fur-
" nifhes many exemples, *fufficient to make us tremble* ; for
" what is more dreadful, than to fee good men fall victims
" to a zeal difpleafing in the fight of God, *and condemned*
" *by the church*, as equally hurtful to religion, and the
" rights of fociety ? the practice of Jefus Chrift, (who dur-
" ing his refidence on earth, bore patiently with the Sadu-
" cees

These truths are now at length generally
known; and they have been of late, so far
publickly

" cees and Samaritans, *the Infidels*, and *Schismatics* of
" those times) obliges us to support our brethren, of what-
" ever communion they be, to live peaceably with them,
" and not to torment them on account of any system of
" belief they have adopted. If we forcibly enlist men
" into the church, we shall only make them prevaricators,
" and hypocrites. The power of the church is purely *spiri-*
" *tual*; and this is so true, that the first Christians suffered
" themselves to be butchered, rather than rebel against the
" edicts of the (Heathen) Emperors: and our blessed Re-
" deemer himself, when he prayed for his executioners,
" *taught us how his cause is to be avenged.* Had the mi-
" nisters of the gospel been always careful to follow that di-
" vine model, the enemies of Christianity had not been able
" to bring against it the unjust reproach of being a perse-
" cutor. The church always *disavowed* those impetuous
" men, who, stirred up by undiscreet zeal, treat those who
" go astray, with asperity; and its most holy bishops, in
" all times, solicited the pardon of apostates, desiring *only*
" *their conversion.* Men, therefore, ought not to impute
" *to the church* those excesses, of which history has preserved
" the memory, and which *are repugnant to the maxims of*
" *the gospel.*" Ganganelli Lett. v. iv. see particularly his
Discourse on the Spirit of the Church, and on Religion.
Passim.

I know Voltaire, that noted scoffer at religion and god-
liness, has written expressly against the authenticity and ge-
nuineness of these letters; but, besides, that the futility of
his objections has already been clearly shewn, by the editor
himself, at the end of the fourth volume; is it at all credi-
ble,

publickly acknowledged, as to have received a kind of fanction from your legislature. A majority of humane and enlightened members in both houses of your Parliament, having been themselves witnesses of the dutiful behaviour of the body of the Roman Catholics of Ireland, under many painful trials: and conscious, that their long perseverance in such behaviour was the best proof of the integrity of that principle, which has hitherto withheld them from sacrificing conscience, and honour to any temporal interest (since rather than violate either by hypocritical professions,) they have, all their lives, patiently suffered in that particular). These truly patriotic members, I say, influenced by such motives, have caused an * oath to be framed (the

ble, that Ganganelli's successor, the present Pope, or his inquisitorial court, which is ever exceedingly vigilant, and jealous on much less important occasions of this kind, would have hitherto suffered such an imposture to remain uncensured, especially, if these letters contained any doctrine repugnant to the essential tenets of the Romish religion?

* In the following words, I A. B do take almighty God, and his only son Jesus Christ, my Redeemer, to witness,

(the moſt certain proof ſurely, that poſ-
ſibly can be required, or given by men, of
the

neſs, that I will be faithful, and bear true allegiance to our
moſt gracious Sovereign Lord, George the third, and him will
defend to the utmoſt of my power, againſt all conſpiracies,
and attempts whatſoever, that ſhall be made againſt his perſon, crown and dignity ; and will do my utmoſt endeavour
to diſcloſe and make known to his majeſty and his heirs, all
treaſons, and traitorous conſpiracies, which may be formed
againſt him or them ; and I do faithfully promiſe to maintain, ſupport, and defend, to the utmoſt of my power, the
ſucceſſion of the crown in his majeſty's family, againſt any
perſon or perſons whatſoever ; hereby utterly renouncing,
and abjuring any obedience or allegiance, to the perſon
taking upon himſelf the ſtile and title of Prince of Wales,
in the life-time of his father ; and who, ſince his death, is
ſaid to have aſſumed the ſtyle and title of King of Great
Britain and Ireland, by the name of Charles the third ; and
to any other perſon claiming, or pretending a right to the
crown of theſe realms. And I do ſwear, that I do renounce and deteſt, as unchriſtian and impious to believe,
that it is lawful to murder, or deſtroy any perſon or perſons
whatſoever, for or under pretence of their being heretics ;
and alſo that unchriſtian, and impious principle, that no
faith is to be kept with heretics. I further declare, that
it is no article of my faith, and I do renounce, reject, and
abjure the opinion that princes excommunicated by the Pope
and council, or by any authority of the See of Rome, or
by any authority whatſoever may be depoſed or murdered
by their ſubjects, or by any perſon whatſoever ; and I promiſe, that I will not hold, maintain or abet any ſuch opinion,

the fincerity of their profeffions) which
without clafhing, in the leaft, with their
religious tenets, fufficiently enfures their
civil duty, and allegiance.

As the conciliating fpirit of the framers
of that oath manifeftly appears in the pre-
amble to it, I fhall take the liberty to in-
infert

nion, or any other opinion contrary to what is expreffed in
this declarations ; and I do declare, that I do not believe
that the Pope of Rome, or any other foreign prince, prelate, ftate, or potentate, hath or ought to have, any temporal or civil jurifdiction, power, fuperiority or pre-emi-
nence, directly, or indirectly, within this realm ; and I do
folemnly, in the prefence of Almighty God, and of his only
fon Jefus Chrift, my Redeemer, profefs, teftify and declare,
that I do make this declaration, and every part thereof, in
the plain and ordinary fenfe of the words of this oath, without any evafion, equivocation, or mental refervation whatever; and without any difpenfation already granted by the
Pope, or any authority of the See of Rome, or any perfon
whatfoever; and without thinking that I am, or can be,
acquitted before God or man ; or abfolved of this declaration, or any part thereof, although the Pope, or any other
perfon or perfons, or authority whatfoever, fhall difpenfe
with, or anull the fame, or declare that it was null and
void from the beginning.

So help me GOD.

sert it here, for your serious and dispassion-
ate revisal.

" Whereas, many of his majesty's sub-
" jects in this kingdom are desirous to tes-
" tify their loyalty and allegiance to his
" Majesty, and their abhorrence of *certain*
" *doctrines imputed to them*; and to remove
" *jealousies,* which hereby have for a length
" of time, subsisted between them, and
" others his Majesty's loyal subjects ; but
" upon account of their religious tenets,
" are by *the laws now in being,* prevented
" from giving public assurances of such
" allegiance, and their *real principles,* good
" will and affection towards their fellow-
" subjects; in order therefore, to give such
" persons an *opportunity of testifying their*
" *allegiance to his Majesty, and good will to-*
" *wards the present constitution of this king-*
" *dom,* and to promote peace and *industry*
" among the inhabitants thereof, be it
" enacted, &c.

This test, so well calculated to answer
all the necessary purposes of civil duty and
allegiance,

allegiance, has, I am affured, been voluntarily and chearfully taken by great and refpectable numbers of the Roman Catholic clergy, nobility, gentry, and people in different parts of that kingdom; whofe example, I doubt not, will be foon followed by thofe few * overfcrupulous perfons,

I

---

* Thefe perfons, however, are not more fcrupulous in this refpect, than feveral members of parliament, firmly attached to the prefent conftitution in church and ftate, feemed to be, who made the like objection to fome part of the wording of this teft, while it was under debate.

Mr. Hercules Langrifhe, in his excellent fpeech in parliament in 1772, on a bill then introduced (but afterwards rejected) to enable Papifts to take building leafes, fays among other things relative to the Popery Laws, " Let us " confider that the time is long fince paft, in which the " recovery of an eftablifhment required *oppreffion for its* " *fupport* ; or the weaknefs of government wifhed to *divide* " *in order to fubdue*. The time is come, in which you " muft offer the Roman Catholics one of thefe two alterna-" tives ; you muft either fuffer them to enjoy the rights of " citizens and fubjects, or do them the juftice to banifh " them from the country. Do not think of flattering them " by the *fupinefs* of laws, which may at any time be re-" vived againft them ; and do not expect their gratitude " becaufe you are not rafh enough to enforce, what you " were *unjuft* enough to enact againft them. Every folid ar-" gument (I wifh I could fay every ideal prejudice too) is " now removed, which might in former times have been

" pleaded

fons, who feem as yet to hefitate at fome part of the wording, but not at the fubftance, or real purport of it.

It

" pleaded againft them——let us not then continue for
" ever to maintain a fyftem of laws—which are tempered
" in the very bigottry of that religion, which they affect
" to reform——which are too fevere to be executed, and
" therefore do not bring fecurity—which, before they can
" operate, muft firft corrupt, which never can be ufeful,
" becaufe they are not juft. Let us not be fo monftrous as
" to fuppofe, we have a right, for ever to preferibe three
" fourths of the community."

While the advocates for the continuance of the Popery laws in a free nation, and under a limited monarchy, vindicate this breach of the public faith, how inconfiftently do they cenfure, as perfidious, the revocation of the edict of Nants, by that abfolute monarch Lewis XIV. whofe will was a law, which the French Proteftants knew they were at all times bound, by the conftitution of their country, implicitly to obey? Of this uncertainty of the French King's edicts, that eminent Proteftant writer, Grotius, was fully fenfible, when on that occafion he faid, " that he earneftly " wifhed fuch edicts might be always religioufly obferved, " but that he would have the Proteftants of France to " know, that they were not to be confidered by them as " treaties or engagements (fœdera) but merely as declara- " tions of that monarch's will and pleafure, made for pu- " blic utility, and revocable by him, when ever the welfare " of the kingdom feemed to require it." Difcuff. Rivetian, apologetic. au. 1645, page 11.

It is therefore, Sir, reasonably to be hoped, that by some favourable change or relaxation of these severe laws; government will make a seasonable acquisition of the hearts and hands of more than a million of zealous and able subjects: now not only an useless, but a wasteful burthen to the public; and, by such just and humane condescention, will prevent all future reproach on your legislature, of countenancing the breach of public faith, of stripping men of their property, for not parting with their integrity, fining and imprisoning them for consciencious dissent from settled forms of worship, or for opinions merely speculative in matters of religion; and in short, of making your protestant courts of justice and equity resemble, in these respects, that hated tribunal a Popish inquisition.

LONDON.   I am, Sir, &c.

P. S.

P. S. A word or two more, and I have done. It has been always declared, by the advocates for the continuance of the Popery Laws, that they were at firſt enacted, and ever ſince kept in force, not on account of the innoxious ſpeculative tenets of Papiſts; but merely as a ſecurity and defence of government, againſt their dangerous practical principles. But ſince theſe *imputed* practical principles are now ſolemnly and explicity abjured; and contrary practical principles as ſolemnly and explicitly avowed by them, in the preſent teſt (which has been propoſed by the legiſlature itſelf, as amply ſufficient for theſe purpoſes) it evidently follows, that the Popery Laws can, now, have no other object, but the innoxious ſpeculative tenets of Papiſts, which it is confeſſed, can afford no juſt cauſe, or even colourable pretence, for that perſecution, and diſtreſs, which theſe laws, by executing themſelves, muſt always, and neceſſarily, bring upon them— On the other hand, what warm returns of gratitude, for the mitigation of theſe laws, may not be expected from a people, whom

whom their unprovoked feverities, for
more than feventy years paft, have not
caufed to deviate from any one duty to
the government that inflicts them? notwithftanding two dangerous * rebellions
have been raifed during that period, in
favour of a Popifh pretender to the crown
of thefe kingdoms; from whofe fuccefs,
they might have reafonably promifed
themfelves fome relaxation, if not an entire abrogation of them. And all the reward I am told, they expect for this fignal
perfeverance in duty and allegiance, is to
be allowed to partake of that common
juftice and chriftian liberty, which even
the fectaries among you, and they not the
beft of fubjects neither, are permitted to
enjoy by the laws of your country, viz.
" a legal toleration to profefs, and openly
" acknowledge, upon every occafion, the
" religion of their confciences, without
" fuffering thereby, any lofs or prejudice,
" either in their perfons or fortunes." And
furely, Sir, that reward cannot in reafon
be longer withheld from them; for, befides

---

* In the year 1715, and 1745.

fides what has been already mentioned; how inconfiftent muft it appear, if the fame government, which confcious of the obligation of public faith, and heedlefs of the clamours of ill defigning men, has granted to the Papifts of Canada (though remote in their fituation, and aliens by birth) the full benefit of their late articles for fuch toleration, fhould ftill continue to deprive thofe of Ireland (who are its natural-born fubjects, refiding in the bofom of the empire, and under its immediate infpection) of thofe advantages, to which they are equally entitled, by the like folemn engagements. Farewell.

London, Sept. 20th, 1777.

THE

THE

CIVIL and MILITARY

A R T I C L E S

O F

L I M E R I C K,

EXACTLY PRINTED FROM THE

LETTERS PATENTS:

WHEREIN

They are ratified and exemplified by their MAJESTIES,
under the GREAT SEAL of ENGLAND.

THE

CIVIL AND MILITARY ARTICLES

OF

LIMERICK.

WILLIAM and Mary, by the Grace of God, &c. *To all* to whom thefe Prefents fhall come, Greeting. *Whereas* certain Articles, bearing Date the third Day of *October* laft paft, Made and Agreed on between Our Juftices of Our Kingdom of *Ireland*, and Our General of Our Forces there on the one Part; and feveral Officers there, Commanding within the City of *Limerick* in Our faid Kingdom, on the other Part. Whereby Our faid Juftices and General did undertake that We fhould ratify thofe Articles, within the Space of eight Months, or fooner; and ufe their utmoft Endeavours that the fame fhould be Ratified and Confirmed in Parliament. The Tenour of which faid Articles, is as follows, *viz.*

A R T I C L E S

Agreed upon the third Day of October, *One Thousand Six Hundred and Ninety One,*

Between the Right Honourable Sir *Charles Porter*, Knight, and *Thomas Conningsby*, Efq; Lords Juftices of *Ireland*; and his Excellency the Baron *De Ginckle*, Lieutenant General, and Commander in Chief of the *English* Army ; *on the one Part.*

And the Right Honourable *Patrick* Earl of *Lucan*, *Piercy* Vifcount *Gallmcy*, Colonel *Nicholas Purcel*, Colonel *Nicholas Cufack*, Sir *Toby Butler*, Colonel *Garret Dillon*, and Colonel *John Brown* ; *on the other Part :*

In the behalf of the *Irifh* Inhabitants in the City and County of *Limerick*, the Counties of *Clare*, *Kerry*, *Cork*, *Sligo*, and *Mayo*.

In Confideration of the Surrender of the City of Limerick, *and other Agreements made between*

between the said Lieutenant General
Ginckle, *the Governor of the City of* Limerick, *and the Generals of the* Irish *Ar-*
my, bearing Date with these Presents,
for the Surrender of the said City, and Sub-
mission of the said Army: It is agreed, That

ART. I. THE *Roman-Catholicks* of this
Kingdom shall enjoy such
Privileges in the Exercise of their Religion,
as are consistent with the Laws of *Ireland;*
or as they did enjoy in the Reign of King
Charles the II. And their Majesties, as
soon as their Affairs will permit them to
summon a Parliament in this Kingdom,
will endeavour to procure the said *Roman-*
Catholicks such further Security in that
Particular, as may preserve them from any
Disturbance upon the Account of their said
Religion.

ART. II. All the inhabitants or Resi-
dents of *Limerick*, or any other Garrison
now in the Possession of the *Irish*, and all
Officers and Soldiers, now in Arms, under
any

any Commiſſion of King *James*, or thoſe
authorized by him, to grant the ſame in the
ſeveral Counties of *Limerick*, *Clare*, *Kerry*,
Cork, and *Mayo*, or any of them ; and all
the Commiſſioned Officers in their Majeſties Quarters, that belong to the *Iriſh*
Regiments, now in being, that are treated
with, and who are not priſoners of War,
or have taken protection, and who ſhall return and ſubmit to their Majeſties obedience ; *and their and every of their Heirs*, ſhall
hold, poſſeſs and enjoy, all and every their
Eſtates of Free-hold, and inheritance : and
all the Rights, Titles and Intereſts, Privileges and Immunities, which they, and every, or any of them held, enjoyed, or were
rightfully and lawfully intitled to, in the
Reign of King *Charles* II. or at any time
ſince, by the Laws and Statutes that were
in Force in the ſaid Reign of King *Charles*
II. and ſhall be put in poſſeſſion, by order
of the Government, of ſuch of them as
are in the King's Hands, or the Hands of
his Tenants, without being put to any ſuit
or trouble therein ; and all ſuch Eſtates
ſhall be freed and diſcharged from all arrears

of

of Crown-rents, Quit-rents, and other publick charges, incurred and become due fince *Michaelmas* 1688, to the day of the date hereof : And all Perfons comprehended in this *Article*, fhall have, hold, and enjoy all their Goods and Chattels, real and perfonal, to them, or any of them belonging, and remaning either in their own hands, or the hands of any perfons whatfoever, in truft for, or for the ufe of them, or any of them : *And all and every the faid perfons, of what Profeffion, Trade, or Calling foever they be,* fhall and may ufe, exercife and practife their feveral and refpective Profeffions, Trades and Callings, as freely as they did ufe, exercife and enjoy the fame in the Reign of King *Charles* II. Provided, that nothing in this *Article* contained, be conftrued to extend to, or reftore any forfeiting perfon now out of the Kingdom, except what are hereafter comprized : Provided alfo, That no perfon whatfoever fhall have or enjoy the benefit of this *Article*, that fhall neglect or refufe to take the Oath of Allegiance, made by act of Parliament

in

in *England,* in the firſt year of the Reign of their preſent Majeſties, when thereunto required.

ART. III. All Merchants, or reputed Merchants of the City of *Limerick,* or of any other Garriſon now poſſeſſed by the *Iriſh,* or of any Town or Place in the Counties of *Clare* or *Kerry,* who are abſent beyond the Seas, that have not bore arms ſince their Majeſties declaration in *February* 1688, ſhall have the benefit of the ſecond article, in the ſame manner, as if they were preſent ; *provided,* ſuch Merchants, and reputed Merchants, do repair into this Kingdom within the ſpace of eight months after the date hereof.

ART. IV. The following Officers, *viz.* Colonel *Simon Lutterel,* Captain *Rowland White, Maurice Euſtace* of *Yermanſtown, Chievers* of *Mayſtown,* commonly called *Mount-Leinſter,* now belonging to the Regiments in the aforeſaid Garriſons and quarters of the *Iriſh* army, who were beyond the Seas, and ſent thither upon affairs

of

of their refpective Regiments, or the *Army* in general, fhall have the benefit and advantage of the fecond article; *provided* they return hither within the fpace of eight months from the date of thefe prefents, and fubmit to their Majefties Government, and take the above mentioned oath.

ART. V. That all and fingular, the faid Perfons comprized in the fecond and third articles, fhall have a general pardon of all Attainders, Outlawries, Treafons, Mifprifions of Treafon, Premunires, Felonies, Trefpaffes, and other Crimes and Mifdemeanors whatfoever, by them, or any of them, committed fince the beginning of the Reign of King *James* II. and if any of them are attainted by Parliament, the Lords Juftices, and General, will ufe their beft endeavours to get the fame repealed by parliament, and the outlawries to be reverfed *Gratis*, all but writing-clerks Fees.

ART. VI. And whereas thefe prefent wars have drawn on great violences on both parts, and that if leave were given to the

bringing

bringing all forts of private actions, the animofities would probably continue, that have been too long on foot, and the publick difturbances laft : for the quieting and fettling therefore of this Kingdom, and avoiding thofe inconveniences which would be the neceffary confequence of the contrary, no Perfon or Perfons whatfoever, comprized in the foregoing articles, fhall be fued, molefted; or impleaded at the fuit of any party or parties whatfoever, for any trefpaffes by them committed, or for any Arms, Horfes, Money, Goods, Chattels, Merchandizes, or Provifions whatfoever, by them feized or taken, during the time of the war. And no Perfon or Perfons whatfoever, in the fecond or third articles comprized, fhall be fued, impleaded, or made accountable for the Rents or mean Rates of any Lands, Tenements, or Houfes, by him or them received, or enjoyed in this Kingdom, fince the beginning of the prefent war, to the day of the date hereof, nor for any wafte or trefpafs, by him or them committed in any fuch Lands, Tenements, or Houfes :

and

and it is alſo agreed, that this article ſhall be mutual, and reciprocal, on both ſides.

ART. VII. Every Nobleman and Gentleman comprized in the ſaid ſecond and third articles, ſhall have liberty to ride with a Sword, and caſe of Piſtols, if they think fit; and keep a Gun in their Houſes, for the defence of the ſame, or for Fowling.

ART. VIII. The inhabitants and reſidents in the city of *Limerick*, and other Garriſons, ſhall be permitted to remove their Goods, Chattels; and Proviſons, out of the ſame, without being viewed and ſearched, or paying any manner of duties, and ſhall not be compelled to leave the Houſes or Lodgings they now have, for the ſpace of ſix weeks next enſuing the date hereof.

ART. IX. The oath to be adminiſtred to ſuch *Roman-Catholicks* as ſubmit to their Majeſties Government, ſhall be the oath aboveſaid, and no other.

ART. X. No Perſon or Perſons, who ſhall at any time hereafter break theſe ar-

L   ticles,

ticles, or any of them, ſhall thereby make, or cauſe any other perſon or perſons, to for-feit or loſe the benefit of the ſame.

ART. XI. The lords juſtices * and ge-neral do promiſe to uſe their utmoſt en-deavours, that all the perſons comprehended in the above mentioned articles, ſhall be protected and defended from all arreſts and executions for debt or damage, for the ſpace of eight months, next enſuing the date hereof.

ART. XII. The lords juſtices and ge-neral do undertake, that their majeſties will ratify theſe articles, within the ſpace of eight months, or ſooner, and uſe their utmoſt endeavours, that the ſame ſhall be ratified and confirmed in parliament.

ART. XIII. Laſtly, And whereas Colo-nel *John Brown* ſtood indebted to ſeveral Proteſtants, by judgments of record; which appearing to the late government, the Lord
Tyrconnel,

* Theſe lords juſtices were then lords of the regency in *Ireland,* as there was no Lord Lieutenant there.

Tyrconnel, and Lord *Lucan*, took away the effects the said *John Brown* had to answer the said debts, and promised to clear the said *John Brown* of the said debts; which effects were taken for the public use of the *Irish*, and their army: for freeing the said Lord *Lucan* of his said engagement, passed on their public account, for payment of the said Protestants, and for preventing the ruin of the said *John Brown*, and for satisfaction of his creditors, at the instance of the Lord *Lucan*, and the rest of the persons aforesaid, it is agreed, that the said lords justices, and the said baron *de Ginckle*, shall intercede with the king and parliament, to have the estates secured to *Roman Catholics*, by articles and capitulation in this kingdom, charged with, and equally liable to the payment of so much of the said debts, as the said Lord *Lucan*, upon stating accompts with the said *John Brown*, shall certify under his hand, that the effects taken from the said *Brown* amount unto; which accompt is to be stated, and the balance certified by the

Lord

Lord *Lucan* in one and twenty days after the date hereof:

For the true performance hereof, we have hereunto set our hands,

Present,	Char. Porter.
Scravemore.	Tho. Coningsby.
H. Maccay.	Bar. De Ginckle.
T. Talmash.	

AND *whereas* the said city of *Limerick* hath been since, in pursuance of the said articles, surrendered unto us, *now know ye*, that we having considered of the said articles, are graciously pleased hereby to declare, that we do for us, our heirs and successors, as far as in us lies, ratifie and confirm the same, and every clause, matter and thing therein contained. And . as to such parts thereof, for which an act of parliament shall be found to be necessary, we shall recommend the same to be made good by parliament, and shall give

our

our royal affent to any bill or bills, that
fhall be paffed by our two Houfes of Parliament to that purpofe. *And whereas* it
appears unto us, that it was agreed between the parties to the faid articles, that
after the words *Limerick, Clare, Kerry,
Cork, Mayo,* or any of them, in the fecond
of the faid articles, the words following,
*viz. and all fuch as are under their protection
in the faid counties,* fhould be inferted, and
be part of the faid articles : which words
having been cafually omitted by the writer,
the omiffion was not difcovered till after
the faid articles were figned, but was taken notice of before the fecond town was
furrendered : and that our faid juftices and
general, or one of them, did promife that
the faid claufe fhould be made good, it
being within the intention of the capitulation, and inferted in the foul draught
thereof : *our further will and pleafure is,* and
we do hereby ratify and confirm the faid
omitted words, viz. [*And all fuch as are
under their protection in the faid counties*]
Hereby for us, our heirs and fucceffors,
ordaining and declaring, that all and every
perfon

perfon and perfons therein concerned, fhall and may have, receive, and enjoy the benefit thereof, in fuch and the fame manner, as if the faid words had been inferted in their proper place, in the faid fecond article; any omiffion, defect, or miftake in the faid fecond article, in any wife notwithftanding. *Provided* always, and our will and pleafure is, that thefe our letters patents fhall be enrolled in our court of *Chancery,* in our faid kingdom of *Ireland,* within the fpace of one year next enfuing. *In witnefs,* &c. *Witnefs* our feal at *Weftminfter,* the twenty-fourth day of *February, anno regni regis & reginæ* Gulielmi & Mariæ *quarto per breve de privato figillo.* Nos *autem tenorem premiffor. prædict. Ad requifitionem attornat. general. domini regis & dominæ reginæ pro regno* Hiberniæ. *duximus exemplificand. per prefentes.* In cujus *rei teftimonium has literas noftras fieri fecimus patentes.* Teftibus *nobis ipfis apud* Weftmon. *quinto die* Aprilis, *annoq. regni eorum quarto.*

BRIDGES.

Examinat. { S. Keck } *In Cancel.*
per nos { Lacon Wm. Childe } *Magiftros.*

The Oath of Fidelity or Allegiance required by the fecond Article of this Treaty,

I. A. B. *do fincerely Promife and Swear, that I will be faithful, and bear true Allegiance to their Majeflies King* William *and* Queen Mary.

So Help me God.

www.ingramcontent.com/pod-product-compliance
Lightning Source LLC
Chambersburg PA
CBHW021426090426
42742CB00009B/1276